11:11

EXPANDED EDITION

By ROBERT M. DRAKE

OTHER BOOKS BY ROBERT M. DRAKE

Spaceship (2012)
The Great Artist (2012)
Science (2013)
Beautiful Chaos (2014)
Beautiful Chaos 2 (2014)
Black Butterfly (2015)
A Brilliant Madness (2015)
Beautiful and Damned (2016)
Broken Flowers (2016)
Gravity: A Novel (2017)
Star Theory (2017)
Chaos Theory (2017)
Light Theory (2017)
Moon Theory (2017)
Dead Pop Art (2017)
Chasing The Gloom: A Novel (2017)
Moon Matrix (2018)
Seeds of Wrath (2018)
Dawn of Mayhem (2018)
The King is Dead (2018)
What I Feel When I Don't Want To Feel (2019)
What I Say To Myself When I Need To Calm The Fuck Down (2019)
What I Say When I'm Not Saying A Damn Thing (2019)
What I Mean When I Say Miss You, Love You & Fuck You (2019)
What I Say To Myself When I Need To Walk Away, Let Go And Fucking Move On (2019)
What I Really Mean When I Say Good-bye, Don't Go And Leave Me The Fuck Alone (2019)
The Advice I Give Others But Fail To Practice My Damn Self (2019)
The Things I Feel In My Fucking Soul And The Things That Took Years To Understand (2019)
Something Broken, Something Beautiful Vol 1(2020)
Something Broken, Something Beautiful Vol 2 (2020)
Something Broken, Something Beautiful Vol 3(2021)
Chasing Moons & Rainbows (2021)
I WROTE THIS FOR YOU ME AND ANYONE TRYING TO FUCKING MOVE ON (2021)
BUT IN THE END YOU JUST HAVE TO LET GO (2022)
OF LOVE AND LIFE (2022)
LOVE STORIES SUCK! (2023)
SHE (2023)
THE LIGHT SHE GIVES (2023)
A BEAUTIFUL MIND (2024)
DETOXIFY(2024)
11:11 (2024)

For Excerpts and Updates please follow:

Instagram.com/rmdrk
Facebook.com/rmdrk
Twitter.com/rmdrk
Tiktok.com/rmdrk
Tumblr.com/rmdrk
Snapchat.com/rmdrk

Book Cover: ROBERT M. DRAKE

"We are beautiful things, wild things,
searching for the brilliance within us."

From the Author:

At times, we must face the storm head-on, embracing the emotions and tears. It's undeniable how unexpectedly pain can find its way to us. Even though we wish to avoid it, it's a part of our journey, deeply etched in our essence, and mirrored in the experiences of others. It's the silent thread that binds us, transcending language and origins. I see your struggle and want you to know you're not isolated. You're destined to navigate this challenge, heal from it, and emerge with even greater vigor. These trials are our pathways to growth, understanding, and the profound lessons of life and affection. While pain might be intrinsic to our existence, and some might feel it more acutely, remember you're never alone. I'm with you, experiencing every emotion, and I promise, clarity will dawn. What's meant for you will always find its way back, mending every fractured piece and bringing every lost fragment home.

11:11

EXPANDED EDITION

By ROBERT M. DRAKE

I wrote this for you. I crafted it with the intention that only you would read it.

Many of us are constantly in search of a sign, a symbol, or a message. Whether it's from above or from someone or something, we seek guidance to point us in the right direction. We desire answers, a hint of the truth we chase. *This is what you've been searching for.*

The intent of this book is not for it to be consumed in one sitting. Instead, when you feel the need for inspiration or direction, randomly open a page. Sometimes the message might seem repetitive, but it's likely because you need to encounter it multiple times. In our fast-paced world, we often forget to prioritize ourselves. We overlook the small joys and moments that offer us peace and clarity.

This book serves as that reminder, guiding you back to the fundamentals, to the very essence.

When someone hurts you, it's a common reaction to want to hurt them in return. However, before you act on that feeling, take a moment to consider what their life might be like. Think about the challenges they might be facing or the reasons behind their actions. Ask yourself if you'd want to be in their position or think and act the way they do. If you wouldn't want to be like them, it's best to let go of the negative feelings. Instead of seeking revenge, wish them well and hope they find peace.

The more you love yourself and give yourself what you need the less you'll demand it from others.

I've become selective about the company I keep. Life has shown me that it's not necessary or beneficial to be friends with everyone. Some people bring unwanted negativity, jealousy, or insincerity into my life. Because of this, I prefer to keep my circle small, surrounding myself only with genuine people, and minding my own business.

True peace comes from understanding that I have the choice to avoid situations or people I don't want in my life. This past year, I've learned a few key things: it's okay to distance myself from certain individuals, accept things as they are without trying to change them, and realize that I don't need to respond to everything. Sometimes, saying less can actually mean a lot more.

It's a beautiful thing when someone continues to love you despite all your complexities and challenges. Having someone who sticks by your side, even when things get tough or you show your flaws, is truly a blessing.

Moving away from a situation and truly letting go are not the same. Running away might mean avoiding a problem or not facing an issue, while letting go means accepting what has happened, finding peace with it, and moving forward without lingering attachments.

People often blame others for problems but overlook their own role in the situation. It's easier to point fingers at someone else than to accept and address our own mistakes or contributions to the issue. It's important to self-reflect and take responsibility for our actions.

When I bring something up, it doesn't mean
I want to fight. I prefer discussing issues
openly and understanding things better. It's
important to remember that as adults, we
should communicate our feelings and
thoughts clearly to avoid misunderstandings.
And to avoid unnecessary arguments.

Have you ever missed someone but felt like
you had to stick to your words or decisions?
It's like being torn between your emotions
and the need to stay true to what you've
previously stated or promised. And still, it
eats you alive in the middle of the night.
Their voice. Their presence. It just hurts.
And what hurts even more is missing them...
while knowing they're no good for you at
all.

Being patient can lead to amazing things. Believe that the Universe has a special plan for you. Even if you can't see it right now, with time, you'll find out that good things come to those who wait and trust in the plan that's stored for you.

Being patient and trusting the journey can lead to great rewards. The Universe has a plan for everyone, and sometimes it takes time to unfold. By waiting and having faith, you might discover wonderful surprises and blessings that you hadn't expected.

Instead of always expecting certain outcomes, try to accept things as they come. By doing so, you'll find that you experience fewer letdowns. When we constantly expect specific things, we set ourselves up for disappointment. Embracing acceptance can lead to a more content and positive outlook on life. And love. And relationships.

Having difficult or complicated talks can lead to stronger, healthier relationships. Instead of dodging these conversations, you should face them head-on. By addressing concerns or misunderstandings, you can build trust and understanding with others, making your bonds even stronger than before.

Stay away from people who only see things from their perspective and fail to understand the feelings and thoughts of others.

Just because someone gives you attention doesn't mean they truly love you. Similarly, feeling attached to someone doesn't necessarily mean there's a deep, genuine connection between you two. And doing just the bare essentials isn't real effort. True love, connection, and effort go beyond superficial actions and feelings; they require genuine care, understanding, and dedication. And I hope it doesn't take a lifetime to understand this.

I once believed that just talking was enough, but I've come to see that understanding is even more crucial. You can talk to someone as much as you want, but if they don't get what you're saying or choose not to grasp it, then all that talking doesn't make a difference. It's essential for both parties to truly understand each other for effective communication. And for an effective relationship. That's all.

Just because you're having a bad day doesn't mean you should take it out on others. It's important for everyone to understand that they shouldn't let their emotions negatively affect the people around them.

The pain didn't give you strength. It hurt you deeply, messed with your emotions, caused sleep problems, made it hard for you to trust, and took away your joy for life. Despite all that, it was your own determination and heart that helped you become stronger. So, remember, the credit goes to you, not the difficult experiences you faced. Although, they taught you a few lessons... it was you who came out of the fire stronger and more resilient than before.

You aren't lazy or lacking drive. You're just tired of the bullshit because you've been constantly trying to cope and get by for a very long time. Living under constant stress and pressure has worn you out, and it's completely understandable to feel this way. In a world that is built to crush you, I can see why you're exhausted from living in high defense mode most of your life.

Healing means learning to appreciate and celebrate the aspects of ourselves that we previously overlooked or undervalued. It's about recognizing our worth, even in the areas we once doubted, and giving ourselves the love and approval we deserve.

Some people will compliment you, saying, "I love your vibe," but then they'll try to take advantage of it or drain it. It's essential to stay alert and recognize when this happens. And stay away from those who try to claim it.

I hope you find a partner who matches your loving and fun nature, and shares the same deep passions and spirituality as you. This person should be open to sharing their deepest thoughts and feelings, and be vulnerable with you in every way. It should feel as if the two of you were meant for each other, like you both wished for one another and it came true.

I don't pull away from people to make them realize something. I do it because I've come to understand and value my own feelings and boundaries. It's about taking care of myself and making sure I'm in a healthy environment.

Choosing to completely shut down and not talk can be as harmful as constantly fighting. Both behaviors can damage relationships because they prevent understanding and resolution. It's essential to communicate and address issues for a healthy relationship.

Breakups can be painful, no doubt. But when you separate from someone who didn't value or respect you, it's actually a good thing. Instead of seeing it as a loss, think of it as gaining the chance for a healthier, happier future without that toxicity in your life.

You don't need to show others how strong you are. Instead, focus on your own well-being and growth. Take it slow, and with each small step you take, learn to find balance and heal yourself. It's okay to progress at your own pace.

Valuing and loving yourself creates a
positive energy or vibe. When you radiate
this kind of positivity, it draws in the things
you desire most, like a magnet. So, treating
yourself with love and care can pave the
way for better experiences and
opportunities.

An easy strategy to enhance your life:
Determine which people deserve your time
and effort, which ones deserve some of your
attention, and which ones shouldn't get any.
It's essential to prioritize relationships and
interactions that truly benefit you and let go
of the ones that don't.

There comes a point when you realize that things usually turn out okay in the end, even if they don't seem like it at the time. This understanding makes you see the importance of believing in yourself and going with the flow, rather than stressing about every little thing.

Tell your daughters that real love doesn't
mean following a man through really tough
times, especially if he's the one causing the
pain. Being with a guy who embarrasses you
for years or cheats on you is not love. It
makes you doubt how valuable you are, and
that's not okay. Giving up your self-respect
to avoid arguments isn't love either. It's
important to unlearn these wrong ideas
about love. A man who truly cares about
you won't do things that could make him
lose you or hurt you in any way.

*One of the worst feelings is pretending to be
okay and holding in all of that pain in front
of the people you love.*

I'm proud of the love I've given to others, even if they didn't return it. Love has a way of coming back to you, maybe in a different way or from a different person. I'll never stop spreading love because I believe it will return to me, even greater than before.

Regardless of how much education you have, the skills you possess, the wealth you've accumulated, or how trendy or popular you feel, the way you behave towards others is the true measure of your heart. Treating people with kindness and respect reveals more about who you truly are than any title or status ever could.

Your attitude plays a crucial role in shaping your experiences. If you view the world positively, it often reflects back the same way. When you remind yourself that you're strong, self-assured, and approach the day with a kind heart, it not only transforms your own experiences but also positively impacts those around you.

Don't be fooled indecisiveness from
someone you want to love. If they can't
make up their mind, that in itself is a choice
they're making. It's important to recognize
when someone is unsure, as it tells you more
about their intentions and shows you how
insecure they are about themselves.

One of the most important lessons I've learned is that we shouldn't cling to relationships or friendships based solely on past memories or the duration we've known someone. If a person doesn't treat you right or respect the bond, it's okay to let them go. Holding on to someone for old times' sake isn't worth it if they aren't contributing positively to your life now.

People often say, "you've changed," as if it's a bad thing. But you know what? They're absolutely correct. I decided it was time to start taking care of myself instead of always putting myself at the bottom of the priority list.

It's not always necessary to get an apology from someone who hurt you in order to heal. Understand that some people find it hard to admit their mistakes. Recognizing this can help you move forward and heal more quickly.

You have to put things into perspective
sometimes and understand how being alone
is better than being used.

Sometimes, simply saying 'I don't want to' is all the reason you need. It's important to listen to your feelings and set limits to protect your heart.

When someone is truly trustworthy, they'll keep your secrets safe, even if you're no longer close or your relationship ends. It's a sign of their genuine character and respect for your trust.

I realized I was maturing when I stopped
letting small problems end my relationships.
I value my relationships a lot, and I've
learned that being in a relationship means
talking about what we expect from each
other and discussing any concerns or issues
we might have. It's about communication
and understanding.

Sometimes you don't get the closure you need and all you are left with is this heavy feeling of wishing you can learn how to unlove someone.

Overthinking is serious. It's not something to laugh about. It can really weigh on you, making you feel consumed and overwhelmed from the inside out.

In your future relationships, try to connect with people who understand themselves or are open to self-improvement. Life is brief, and it's not worth repeating old relationship problems with new partners. Seek out those who learn and grow from their experiences.

It's not just about who shows interest in you at first; it's more about who consistently chooses and prioritizes you over time, showing their commitment every day.

Big respect goes to those who are working hard to change their toxic habits. If you're putting in the effort to improve your mental health and become the best you can be, you deserve praise. Keep going; it's a big deal to actively change and grow into a better version of yourself.

When we feel unhappy, sometimes it's because of our own negative thoughts and attitudes. It's easy to focus on the bad things and forget the good in our lives. Instead of dwelling on the negatives, try to focus on the positive aspects. Think about all the good things you have and the happy moments you've experienced. Remember to be grateful and express your thanks to the universe. When you show gratitude, you open yourself up to more blessings and positivity in your life.

A narcissist often doesn't take responsibility for their actions. If you confront them about something bad they've done to you, they're likely to hold a grudge. Instead of admitting their mistakes, they might get upset with you for pointing them out and may not forgive you for it. This is because they typically have a hard time accepting that they could be at fault.

It's important to make sure people are responsible for being hurtful to us, regardless of the topic of the lie. Often, people lie to control situations or get something they want. They might lie believing they won't be caught or because they're scared of losing us if they're truthful. Over time, if they see that we forgive their dishonesty easily, they might feel they can deceive us about even bigger things without consequences. It's all about them taking advantage of the trust and love we've shown them.

When you started to love the narcissist, they acted like a reflection of you, imitating your behaviors and interests to win you over. However, if you start noticing they're changing in appearance, behavior, or speech, it might be because they've found a new person to mimic. This new person is their new focus, and they're adapting to this individual just like they did with you at the start.

When someone says they love you before they really know your daily habits and quirks, they might have ulterior motives. If they quickly include you in major life events, introduce you to their family, or even have you dine with their children within the first month, they're likely rushing things for a reason. Similarly, if they talk about building a life together very early on, it might not be a genuine plan. In all these situations, they might have a hidden agenda, and the fast-paced relationship might not be as real as it seems.

When you unexpectedly fall in love with someone you never planned to, it's a special kind of love. There's no need to force a connection or try to change them. It's just a genuine bond that naturally forms between you two, making it pure and authentic.

Many individuals don't pretend to have depression; instead, they often hide their true feelings and act as if everything is fine. It's essential to keep this in mind and show compassion, as you may not know what someone is silently going through. Always treat others with kindness and understanding.

Sometimes, it's good to take a step back and not let emotions control you. Life can be easier and less stressful when you don't get caught up in every little thing or worry about what others think.

If someone doesn't recognize your worth or appreciates you, it's not your job to persuade them. Everyone deserves to be with people who see their true value and cherish them for who they are. Instead of trying to change their minds, focus on those who genuinely value and support you.

Often, individuals with the kindest hearts
and most genuine intentions have faced the
harshest treatment from others. They've felt
the sting of rejection, betrayal, loneliness,
and abandonment. Because they've been
through such pain, they understand deeply
how it feels. This is why they strive to treat
others with kindness and compassion,
knowing firsthand the impact of hurtful
actions.

She is strong but she hurts too. She just chooses to do it silently and when no one is watching.

People who are smart in school or work are unique, but finding someone who understands and handles emotions well is even harder to find. Wouldn't everyone want a friend or partner like that? Imagine having someone by your side who gets your emotions, treats them with kindness, and has patience. It's so reassuring to be with someone you can be open with, and they respond with genuine understanding. That's the true value of emotional intelligence.

At this point in my life, I'm focused on healing from past hurts, continuously improving myself, maintaining consistent routines, seeking stability in all areas, finding my true calling, and achieving inner peace. I want to prioritize things that truly matter and bring positive change to my life.

Don't betray your girlfriend's trust, especially when she has turned down others to be with you. It's important to recognize the sacrifices she's made and the commitment she's shown by choosing you over others. Being loyal and appreciating her choice builds a stronger, more trusting relationship.

You're an adult with your own thoughts and decisions. You don't need to constantly justify your actions or choices to others. Stand confident in who you are and remember that you don't owe everyone an explanation for everything you do.

Healing doesn't mean you'll always feel joy.
It means that when you face tough times or
sadness, you have the experience and
understanding to manage your feelings and
get back to a balanced state. It's about
coping and adapting, not constant happiness.

Just texting doesn't capture everything. Let's sit under the moonlight together, watch the stars, and have a real conversation about life and our dreams.

Your 20s are like a wild ride full of ups and downs. During this time, you might drift apart from some friends and even lose touch with family members. You might also go through breakups that make you really sad. But it's also a time for learning about who you are. You'll start to understand why you act a certain way, often because of things that happened when you were a kid. There will be happy times too—you'll laugh a lot and meet new people who might become close friends. You'll change and get stronger, and along the way, you'll figure out some of the things you really want in life.

Even after they hurt you and left you
shattered, you still hope for their happiness.
This deep compassion and ability to forgive
showcases the incredible strength and
kindness of your heart. It truly says a lot
about the beautiful person you are,
especially when faced with challenges and
pain. And i hope you never change.

Overthinkers often anticipate pain or disappointment. So, if you try to hurt them, you're not surprising them. Instead, you're just confirming what they had already imagined in their minds, making them feel they were right from the very start.

You made the decision to leave, and that was your choice. But I had to make my own choice too, and that was to accept it and let you move on. It wasn't easy, but it was something I felt I had to do.

Sometimes spending the night with the right person can feel like a lifetime together.

Stay hydrated by drinking plenty of water. Take a moment to meditate and find inner peace. Take care of your skin by using moisturizers. Eat delicious and juicy fruits for a boost of energy and health. Enjoy relaxing, extended showers to refresh yourself. Stretch your body and take deep breaths to relieve tension. Dive into captivating books to expand your mind. Think about starting your own business venture. Stay focused on your own life and avoid unnecessary drama. Love people without any conditions or expectations. Always communicate how you feel openly. Explore and learn from different cultures and languages. Let yourself experience emotions fully. Try to understand situations and people better. Express yourself by creating art in any form. Remember to forgive those who hurt you and work on your own healing process.

I really appreciate people who find joy in simple things like enjoying the rain, the glow of the moon, autumn leaves, a night full of stars, or an engaging conversation. These are the kind of people who see beauty in everyday moments and cherish the little things in life.

Being in a relationship is about understanding and caring for our partner's unique needs and feelings. It's not just about doing what's easy or convenient for us. It means making an effort to support and love them in the specific ways they appreciate, even if it takes us out of our comfort zone.

Avoid people who don't value the small gestures you offer, whether it's spending money you might not have to spare, buying meals, offering rides, or just giving kind words. Even things like offering a listening ear, being the first to initiate contact, or boosting their confidence matter. Sadly, some folks only see what benefits they can get from you. Some might even use your assistance but prioritize helping others, overlooking the person who's genuinely supporting them - which is you. Remember, it's essential to surround yourself with those who genuinely appreciate your efforts.

At times, your mind might take longer to come to terms with something your heart understands right away. This means that even if you feel something deep down, your thoughts might need more time to process and truly accept it.

It's been a few years since I last saw you and sometimes when I think about you...I can't help but to feel... A little sad.

Sometimes, problems don't have clear answers. Finding peace often means understanding and accepting that certain situations won't change, no matter how much we wish they would. It's about letting go and making peace with things as they are.

People relate to your experiences based on how well they understand their own life challenges. This means if someone hasn't faced something similar or hasn't taken the time to reflect on their experiences, they might not fully grasp what you're going through. They might not fully understand.

Fixing trust in a relationship needs both people to be on board. If one person isn't genuinely sorry, forgiving them might not make things better. Pretending like nothing happened doesn't heal the hurt. And if you keep trusting someone who keeps breaking that trust, you'll likely face the same issues again and again.

We often idealize the idea of 'forever' in love, believing it's the ultimate truth. However, some of the most touching and powerful love stories of our generation are those that show us the importance and beauty of learning to move on and letting go.

Narcissists often have a double standard
when it comes to rules and behavior. For
them, others are expected to constantly
apologize, show them utmost respect, and
avoid any criticism or disagreement.
Additionally, they expect others to obey
their commands and suppress their own
emotions. Yet, they don't follow these rules
themselves. Narcissists often feel entitled to
act as they please, speak without thinking of
the consequences, and show disrespect.
Even though they avoid apologizing, they
see their actions as acceptable.

When women are truly loved and treated
with kindness and respect, it has a noticeable
impact on them. They radiate confidence,
happiness, and positivity. This glow is not
just physical but emotional too. Being in a
nurturing and supportive environment
allows them to flourish, leading to an overall
sense of well-being and contentment. This
genuine love and proper treatment can bring
out the best in them, making them shine
brighter in every aspect of life.

Every person should spend some time being
totally on their own. This means not relying
on messages or calls from others, handling
all responsibilities like bills by themselves,
treating themselves well, and spending time
on self-improvement like working out or
practicing mindfulness through prayer or
meditation. This experience is valuable
because it builds inner strength. When
someone learns how to be comfortable on
their own, they won't settle for less than they
deserve out of fear of loneliness. Someone
who's learned to be content alone won't put
up with unnecessary drama or disrespect,
because they know their own worth.

Sometimes you actually understand what needs to be done or what is true, but you're not emotionally prepared to admit it to yourself. In other words, deep down you know what the right choice or answer is, but you might be scared or hesitant to face that reality. It's like you're holding back from accepting what you already know is true.

Sometimes people don't pay attention to your emotional well-being until it gets to a point where you can't hold in your feelings anymore and you get angry. Once that happens, others may start to view you as a difficult person, even though the real issue is that you've been struggling mentally for a while and no one noticed or helped.

When you're a really good person, with a kind heart and pure soul, you're not the one who misses out if people walk away from you. Actually, it's those people who are losing something valuable. They're missing the chance to have someone truly caring and genuine in their lives. This can be hard to understand, especially when you're the one left behind, but it's important to remember that your goodness is a gift that not everyone is ready to appreciate. Nor deserving of it.

If you're trying to decide between being with me or being with someone else, it's better if you don't pick me. This might sound strange, but the point is that if you really have to think hard about who to choose, then maybe I'm not the right choice for you to begin with. In relationships, you want to be with someone who knows for sure that they want to be with you, without any doubts. So if you're stuck deciding, go ahead and pick the other person.

Don't waste your time running after people who don't want to be in your life. If they block you, stop talking to you, or don't pay attention to you, it's better to just let them go. Instead, focus on the people who genuinely enjoy spending time with you and like you for who you are. We often try too hard to keep people in our lives, worrying that they'll leave us. But the people who really matter are the ones who choose to stick around without being pressured or chased. Appreciate them, because they're the ones who really value you. They are the ones who stay.

Getting better after feeling mentally, emotionally, or physically drained can take a really long time, sometimes years. Even if you begin to rest more and live a less stressful life, your body and mind don't forget what you've been through. The stress or emotional pain you felt in the past can still affect you. It's important to know this so you can be kind to yourself. Take your time, be patient, and don't rush the healing process. You need to give yourself the space and time you need to fully recover. Stay strong.

Don't let other people's actions control your life or how you feel. If someone doesn't call you, it's okay—just go to bed and get some rest. If you're not getting a text back, put your phone down and focus on enjoying your day. If someone is acting cold or distant and won't explain why, it's fine to go home and do something that makes you happy. Remember, you should put yourself first and take care of your own well-being. Other people come second, so don't let their actions ruin your day or your mood.

Between the ages of 25 and 30, many people
begin to feel a greater sense of responsibility
and concern about various aspects of their
lives. This might include thinking about
their long-term career goals, planning for
their financial future, or pondering about
finding the right life partner. Additionally,
during this time, there's often a deeper
appreciation for parents. As we mature, we
recognize that our parents are aging and
won't be around forever, which can lead to a
heightened sense of gratitude for all they've
done and the time we have with them.

It's fine to joke around, but making fun of someone's insecurities is not fun. When you joke about how someone looks, thinks, feels... you might think it's funny, but it can hurt their feelings. It's always good to think before you speak. Imagine how the other person would feel if you made fun of something they are sensitive about. We should aim to be kind and considerate, so everyone can enjoy a good laugh without feeling picked on. Without feeling attacked.

That's the thing, once you catch feelings for someone it's really hard to stop. Even if in the middle of it all you find out they're no good for you.

I believe it's crucial for us to have clear
criteria for our friendships. Instead of
choosing friends based on looks, it's more
important to consider their way of thinking.
We should surround ourselves with friends
who are open-minded and respectful. As we
grow older, it's not healthy to spend time
with individuals who are narrow-minded
and inconsiderate. We deserve better and
should prioritize our well-being.

It's not only about communication, but understanding each other's viewpoints is just as crucial. If I share my feelings with you and you don't try to see things from my perspective, it makes me wonder why I should even bother sharing. It's not just about hearing the words; it's about truly listening and trying to get where the other person is coming from. Otherwise, the essence of communication is lost.

A sincere conversation and a genuine apology can mend many problems, but some individuals lack the maturity to have those hard and difficult discussions. Often, misunderstandings or issues can be resolved by simply communicating openly and vulnerably. However, not everyone has the ability or willingness to confront issues head-on, take responsibility, or discuss feelings. This maturity can make a big difference in relationships and problem-solving. Sometimes a conversation is all you need to mend a broken heart.

My last relationship taught me: you can be the perfect person for the wrong person.

You shouldn't feel guilty for moving forward if you've given someone multiple opportunities to improve or change, but they didn't. Everyone has limits, and it's important to look out for your own well-being. If you tried to help or waited for them to change their behavior, but things stayed the same, it's okay to choose what's best for you and move on. Prioritizing your own happiness and peace is essential, especially when you've been patient and understanding for a long time.

Everyone deserves a love where the other person understands and acknowledges their feelings. When someone says, "I'm sorry you feel that way," it can feel like they're dismissing your feelings. But when someone says, "I'm sorry for how I made you feel," it means they're taking responsibility for their actions and genuinely care about how you feel. It's important to have someone in your life who genuinely recognizes and apologizes for their mistakes, showing that they value your emotions and the relationship.

True love is when someone is there for you during the tough times, not just the good ones. It's easy for someone to be with you when everything is going well. But if they stay by your side when things get difficult, it shows they genuinely care. Love is tested in challenges, formed through hardship and kept through building bonds... and those who stay, stay with you through them because they deeply love you and believe in you no matter what.

When you're thinking about breaking up
from a relationship that's not good for you,
don't only think about the difficulties of
ending it. Think deeply about the problems
and pain you face by staying in it. For
example, staying might mean more hurt
feelings, stress, or lost opportunities. When
you really compare the problems from
staying with the challenges of leaving, it
might become clearer that leaving is the
better choice. It's like comparing the weight
of two bags: if one is much heavier and
harder to carry, you'd likely want to put it
down.

There will come a time when you'll feel
strong enough to deal with the tough
feelings you've been avoiding. When that
time comes, be brave and stand your ground.
Remember, even if you achieve many great
things, it doesn't mean you can skip the
healing process. Healing is important, no
matter how successful you are. Everyone
needs to face their feelings and find peace
and clarity within them.

Sometimes people hurt you by making a one-time mistake, and other times people hurt you by repeating the same hurtful actions again and again. Mistakes are usually easier to forgive because they are not done on purpose and everyone makes them sometimes. However, when someone repeatedly does something hurtful, it's a pattern that shows they may not be willing to change their behavior. It's important to recognize the difference between these situations. Forgiving a mistake can help a relationship grow, but it might be necessary to take action to stop a harmful pattern, which might include having a serious discussion or even reconsidering the relationship.

Being open and showing your true feelings can connect you with others. When you share your own experiences and emotions, it helps others see that they're not the only ones going through tough times or feeling certain ways. It creates a bond, making people feel understood and less alone in their struggles. Sharing can be a way to bring people together and support each other. Just don't be afraid of opening your heart and don't be afraid of letting people in.

Being patient with yourself makes you stronger. It helps you see things more clearly and understand the world better. When you take your time and don't rush, you can spot chances and opportunities that you might have missed if you were hurrying. So, by slowing down and being gentle to yourself, you open up more possibilities for good things to come your way.

No matter how lonely you feel...
understand... that you are never quite alone.
The universe is always with you.
Comforting you with its suns, moons and
stars... hugging everything about you that
hurts.

Just because someone says they love you doesn't mean they can have a successful relationship with you. Being in a relationship needs more than just love. It requires both people to be open emotionally, to be ready to work on the relationship, and to have good communication skills. So, when you're looking for a lasting relationship, find someone who's ready to work on building a strong bond, not just someone who says they have feelings for you.

Let go of trying to be perfect or doing things just to show off. Don't set goals just because you want to look good in front of others. It's okay if you don't always stand out or if things aren't always big and flashy. Decide for yourself what success means, and you'll see a positive change in your life much quicker. Focus on what truly matters to you and not on what others think.

Being kind doesn't mean you always have to please everyone. It's possible to show kindness while still setting boundaries for yourself. Similarly, being generous doesn't require you to give up everything or put yourself at a disadvantage. You can offer help and share with others in ways that don't harm your own well-being. Lastly, loving others doesn't mean neglecting yourself. You can care deeply for others, but it's also important to show the same love and care to yourself.

If someone isn't putting in the effort, don't waste your energy trying even harder to please them or get their attention. Think of it like a friendship where you're always the one calling or making plans, but the other person rarely shows up or cancels often. Instead of trying even harder to make it work, it might be better to slowly step back and focus on those who value and appreciate your time and effort. If all you see from someone is that they can't be consistent, it's okay to start reevaluating the entire relationship. Sometimes it's not meant to work out and sometimes it's okay to move on.

Believe in the decisions you've made for
your life. It's okay if you don't get
everything perfect from the start. Making
mistakes is a natural part of learning and
growing. When you mess up, you learn from
it. Those lessons from your mistakes help
shape you into the best version of yourself.
So, even when things don't go as planned,
remember that each setback is guiding you
towards who you're meant to be.

It's okay to have feelings, make mistakes,
and not be perfect all the time. That's just
being human. Everyone is like this, and it's a
natural part of who we are. You shouldn't
feel bad about it. Nobody is perfect, no
matter how hard they try. Instead of
focusing on being perfect, it's better to
appreciate and find the good things in our
unique qualities and mistakes. They make us
who we are, and there's something special
and beautiful about that.

Keep going and follow your plan. You knew from the start that it wouldn't be a walk in the park. To reach higher goals, you need to work hard, stay focused, and sometimes give things up. As you aim for bigger things, the challenges can get tougher. But, when the moment comes for you to shine, you'll be glad you didn't give up and stayed true to your path.

You're the first person who can protect yourself from things or people that try to pull you off track. Be careful about who and what you let into your life. Think of your mind and energy as treasures, and keep them safe. Make sure you stay focused and don't let anyone take advantage of you. Nor drain you of your energy.

Be good to yourself today. If you start
feeling anxious, keep in mind that just
because you feel a certain way doesn't mean
it's true. If you start doubting yourself and
feel like you don't belong or aren't good
enough, push through that fear. You can still
move forward even if you're scared. And if
you feel like everything has to be perfect,
just remember that finishing something is
often more important than making it perfect.
It's okay to do your best and let it be. Don't
be too hard on yourself; everyone has these
feelings sometimes.

When you come across people who bring
negativity into your life, it's okay to distance
yourself from them without giving any
explanations. You don't owe them any
goodbyes. It's alright to delete their phone
numbers and messages from your phone.
You can also stop following them on social
media, or even unfriend and block them if
necessary. Doing this helps to keep them out
of your life. It's important to surround
yourself with positive influences because
you deserve better. It's all about taking steps
that contribute to your own happiness and
well-being. Sometimes, removing negative
individuals from your life is a necessary step
towards creating a more positive and healthy
environment for yourself to grow.

Don't act one way with someone and feel another, it can confuse them. It's fucked up to make someone think they're important to you if you can't really be there for them. If you don't really like someone, stop pretending to like them. If you're not ready for a serious relationship, be honest about it. Tell them directly or take a step back. Everyone deserves to know the truth so they can feel at peace, rather than being left with sadness, confusion and chaos.

It's okay to sometimes get overwhelmed by your feelings. Everyone, being human, feels strong emotions at times. There might be moments when you react strongly because of these emotions. But remember, feelings can be intense but they don't last forever. Once things calm down and you feel clearer, you can always take a moment, reflect, and find your balance again. It's all a part of being human, and you can always find your way back to feeling centered.

It's important to be understanding and patient with yourself. Think about when you were younger or didn't know as much - it's okay that you made mistakes or didn't have all the answers. Be gentle with yourself today, especially as you work hard to change old habits that you now know aren't good for you. And for the future you, always do your best with what you have now. This way, you're setting up a kinder, brighter future for yourself. Remember, always treat yourself with kindness no matter where you are in life.

Mindfulness is like medicine for your mind. It helps stop too many thoughts from spinning around in your head and keeps you from feeling overwhelmed. If you start worrying about what's coming next, try to bring yourself back to what's happening right now. Pay attention to what you can see, hear, or feel in this moment. By concentrating on the present, you can feel more calm and centered. This will help you find balance. It will help you feel like yourself again.

Loving someone without conditions doesn't mean they get unlimited access to your life or time. Just like a garden needs fences to protect it, even the most loving relationships need boundaries to keep them healthy. It's okay to set limits and rules in relationships, and it's actually a sign of a true and caring love. When we set boundaries, it shows that we respect ourselves and the other person, ensuring that the relationship remains strong and positive.

It's tough to stop trying to please everyone, especially when you've been taught to act this way for a long time. Growing up, someone might have made you feel that expressing your thoughts or feelings could lead to problems or conflict. This might be why you've often kept quiet or put others' needs before your own. But remember, as you start to speak up and find your own voice again, it's important to be patient and gentle with yourself. It's a journey of self-discovery and self-love, and you deserve support and understanding along the way.

Keep going and take care of yourself.
Continue to heal and give yourself the love
and care you need. This is not just for your
own well-being, but also for those around
you who will benefit from the stronger and
better person you're becoming. Remember,
you have a special place in this world and
people who value you. You're important and
make a difference.

Here's a simple truth: life feels better when
you spend time doing things you love.
Sometimes, life's challenges can make you
feel down or take away your happiness. But
remember, you have the power to control
how much it affects you. It's like setting
aside a special spot in your day just for
things that make you smile. Think of it as
saving a piece of chocolate for yourself in a
big box of assorted candies. You deserve
that treat! So, make sure you regularly do
things that bring you joy. Make your
happiness a top priority. It's important to
have something to look forward to,
especially during tough times.

Sometimes people say, "Don't worry, it's not that big of a deal." But sometimes, it really feels like a big deal. Feelings can be overwhelming, and it's okay if you need time to understand them. Imagine your emotions like a big puzzle; you can't always solve it right away. Taking time to sort through your feelings doesn't mean you're not strong. It just means you're human, and like everyone else, you need a moment to figure things out.

Here's a simple way to think about it:
Growing and changing can feel tough, like
trying on a pair of new shoes that haven't
been broken in yet. It pushes you, maybe
even challenges you more than you're used
to. It can feel tiring while you're going
through it, just like a workout. But, in the
end, just like how those shoes eventually fit
perfectly, or how exercise makes you
stronger, the growth you experience is truly
rewarding.

You should have relationships where love is the main ingredient, not jealousy. Your friends should genuinely want good things for you. Sometimes, this might mean taking a break from each other, like how plants need space to grow. You deserve to be surrounded by people who genuinely support and celebrate your success, not just those who stick around thinking they'll get something out of it. Think of it like having true fans in your life, not just people looking for a free ticket to the show.

Don't try too hard to get close to someone who clearly isn't interested in you. Even if you have strong feelings for them, it's important to value yourself. Some people might still treat you with respect, but others might see it as an opportunity to take advantage of you. Stay calm and collected, avoid appearing too desperate, and don't do things that might harm you or your self-worth.

Many people discuss the idea of ending relationships or distancing themselves from others, but few address the deep sadness and pain that accompanies such decisions. It's tough to stay committed to that choice, especially when it's not what your heart desires, but when you know it's essential for your own mental and emotional health.

Communication is key because it helps us understand the real situation, rather than just what we imagine or assume. By talking openly, we can clarify misunderstandings, avoid jumping to conclusions, and ensure we're on the same page. Without good communication, we might believe stories we've created in our heads, which can lead to unnecessary confusion or conflict.

People who were taught as kids that their needs matter often find it easier to communicate and see their needs as fair. However, those who often aim to please others, depend too much on someone, or have trouble setting limits might doubt their feelings or needs. They've grown up thinking they shouldn't ask for too much. So, when someone tells them they're "asking for too much" or being "too needy," it makes them feel like their past experiences were right. It strengthens the idea that they should put others' needs before their own and keep their feelings to themselves.

I'm not looking for a perfect relationship. I just want someone who puts in the same effort and commitment as I do. It's important to me that both of us work together to make the relationship bloom.

It's hard to have a healthy relationship with someone who doesn't own up to their mistakes. In a strong partnership, both people need to acknowledge when they're wrong and work towards making things right. If someone consistently avoids taking blame or making amends, it creates trust issues and can lead to bigger problems down the road. For a relationship to thrive, both partners need to be accountable for their actions and willing to grow from them.

If someone doesn't recognize any issues
with their behavior, they're unlikely to
change. Remember this before spending a
lot of time hoping someone will change
when they truly don't see a problem. It's
tough, if not impossible, to alter someone's
mindset or perspective. If their behavior is
hurting you and they don't understand or
acknowledge it, it might be best to walk
away for your own well-being. Sometimes,
prioritizing yourself and finding a healthier
environment is the best thing to do... even if,
at first... it causes you a little pain.

If a man constantly uses his past pain or struggles as a reason to hurt you, it's hard to help him heal. Think about it: if someone keeps justifying their harmful actions because of their past, they're not really taking responsibility for how they treat you now. You deserve someone who treats you well, regardless of their history. It's important to prioritize your well-being and be cautious of those who repeatedly blame their past for current hurtful behavior.

Your partner should be someone you can rely on and feel at ease with, not another source of stress or conflict in your life. A relationship should be a sanctuary where both of you support and uplift each other. If you constantly feel like you're fighting or at odds with your partner, it's not the nurturing and comforting relationship you deserve. It's essential to have a partner who makes life easier, not harder.

*I been fucked over so many times that when
I finally meet someone who cares it scares
the hell out of me! I don't know what to do...*

Many believe depression is just about feeling sad and shedding tears often, but for me, it's like being lost in a never-ending dusk. It's when my mind goes blank, and I find myself unresponsive and indifferent to everything around me. I'm not necessarily sad; I just feel hollow, as if all the color has drained from the world. I experience many days filled with this numbing emptiness, and they are incredibly challenging to get through.

Avoid returning to situations or relationships that once caused you pain and required you to seek healing. Revisiting them can reopen old wounds and hinder your progress.

It's perfectly fine if your life's ambitions have shifted to embrace a quieter, perhaps smaller-scale existence than you once envisioned. If you discovered that your original goals were more daunting than you could handle and you've chosen a more manageable direction, it's okay. It's also okay if the passion you thought would drive your life turned out not to be your true calling and you've since ventured into new territories. And if you're currently in a phase where your previous aspirations don't seem right but you're unsure of the next step, that's okay. Trust that you'll find your way eventually.

Let go of anything or anyone that has let go of you. Holding on only keeps you from moving forward.

When a partner avoids sharing your relationship
publicly or acknowledging it openly, it might be
a sign of infidelity or that they are keeping their
options open with others. Excuses like avoiding
drama or not wanting others involved often
don't hold up, as many people take pride in
sharing their relationship with the world. There's
a fine line between privacy and secrecy; if you're
hidden, it could be that they fear losing
opportunities with someone else, indicating a
lack of commitment. It's important to recognize
whether you're being protected or kept as a
secret.

Claiming to love someone while treating them poorly is a form of mental and emotional harm. This behavior should stop because it's damaging and deceitful. Love should be reflected in actions, not just words. It creates a cycle of confusion and pain, making the person on the receiving end question their worth and reality. True love involves respect, kindness, and consistent care, so if the actions don't align with the declarations of love, it's not just misleading—it's destructive.

If my partner tends to worry too much, I'll make sure to provide clear explanations. I'm completely okay with taking the time to reassure them. The aim is to create a foundation of trust, not to break it down.

If a person retreats from a relationship when facing demands or expectations, it might not be that your needs are too great, but rather that they're not prepared to meet them. Strength in a partner is shown by their willingness to work through challenges, not escape to easier situations.

It's not fair to accuse someone of having trust issues if you've given them reasons to doubt you, especially if you've lied to them before. Trust is built on honesty, and without it, doubt and mistrust are natural responses.

Partners who offer emotional stability and make decisions with understanding and insight will experience the most tender, genuine, and nurturing sides of their significant other. When someone feels emotionally safe and guided with wisdom, they are more likely to be open, trusting, and supportive in the relationship.

If someone begins to disregard you, it's best to step away silently. There's no need to send lengthy messages of frustration or signs in hopes of making them realize what they're losing. Forget the thoughts that they won't find another you or that they'll be filled with regret. Gather yourself and go. You are worthy of a love that never doubts your value right from the start.

Pay attention to how they act when someone challenges them, disagrees with them, or sets limits. Their behavior in these moments will show you their true nature.

Find yourself a partner who supports your well-being in every aspect: your mind, body, and soul. Look for someone patient, kind, and empathetic, someone who meets your efforts with equal enthusiasm and who loves you sincerely and without conditions. Choose someone who sees the best in you and is committed to keeping that brightness alive, who encourages you to shine brighter.

A person who doesn't value themselves often doesn't know how to accept the affection given to them. They may even be unkind to someone who offers them love. It's like they can't believe they're worthy of care, so they react badly to those who try to give it. When someone truly loves themselves, they can love others better and treat them with the kindness that everyone deserves.

If we aren't able to support each other in becoming better and achieving more, then it's important for us to move on separately. This means if we're not making positive changes in each other's lives, encouraging one another, and learning from each other, then it might be healthier for us to end our relationship or friendship. It's essential for people to contribute to each other's personal development. If that's not happening, holding on might hold us back, so sometimes, going our own ways is the best choice.

Don't worry too much. Keep being you and
know that soon enough the universe will expose
all the wrong people have done to you.

It's such a great feeling when you finish a conversation with someone and you're left with this warm, happy feeling inside because the talk was really positive and it brightened your day. It's like your mind got a little lighter and your heart a little fuller because of the uplifting and insightful things you both shared. It's one of the best feelings out there.

There are moments when things go your way and you get exactly what you've been hoping for. But there are also times when instead of getting what you want right away, you end up learning valuable things. You might learn to wait patiently because not everything happens immediately. You could understand that sometimes the timing isn't right, and you have to wait for the right moment. You may also discover how to see things from someone else's point of view, which is empathy, or you might develop a deeper sense of kindness and a desire to help others, which is compassion. Sometimes you learn to keep believing even when it's tough—that's faith. Perseverance is when you keep going despite the obstacles, and resilience is your ability to bounce back from setbacks. Humility can come from realizing you're not always going to be first or best, and trust develops when you learn to rely on others or believe that things will work out. You might find deeper meaning in your life or become more aware of yourself and your surroundings. You may face challenges that make you stronger, which is resistance, or discover your true purpose. Clarity can come when you finally understand something that was confusing before. And even in sadness or grief, you can find beauty and appreciate life more deeply. No matter which of these experiences come your way, you end up gaining something valuable. So, in the end, you always come out ahead.

I genuinely wish for you to discover a person
who becomes essential to your existence,
someone whose presence is so pivotal that the
mere thought of being apart is unimaginable.
And with all my heart, I hope you'll never
experience the pain of having to endure life in
their absence. May you find that soul-connecting
companionship that enriches every moment, and
may you be spared the anguish of separation, for
to love profoundly is to recognize how
irreplaceable some people become. May your
journey be blessed with enduring togetherness,
and the trials of parting never touch your
doorstep.

Even as paths diverge, it doesn't erase the history of growing together. Our shared experiences have intertwined our lives in a way that time or distance cannot fully untangle. This bond, formed from shared growth, is something I'll always cherish. It's comforting to know that, despite the different directions we've taken, the roots of our relationship remain interlaced. They hold the memories of our closeness, and no matter where we go from here, that connection, once so vital, has left a permanent imprint on who we are.

We could have had it all: a whole life together,
kids, a house, two dogs—the whole nine yards.
We could have spent the rest of our lives holding
each other to sleep, making each other laugh,
growing old together, and making our dreams
come true. We could have had that, and I know
it could have worked out. Perhaps knowing this
is the hardest thing of all.

In life, you'll meet individuals who seem to always know exactly what to say when to say it. However, it's not their well-timed words but their deeds that truly reveal their character. What they do, rather than what they say, is what really counts. Pay attention to how their promises align with their actions, how their commitments are reflected in their day-to-day behavior. Over time, actions paint a true portrait of a person's intentions and values, far beyond the fleeting impressions of charming words.

Your presence in my life was not just about love; you were the companion who brought out the best in me, and the thought of losing that again is unfathomable. Perhaps it's hard for you to grasp, but what I offered you was my utmost self, and ever since you've been gone, everything has changed.

Choose a partner who aspires to the mutual commitment of marriage, rather than one who is simply seeking a spouse. A dedicated partner is ready to contribute, care, and uphold each other's rights, striving to make the relationship thrive. In contrast, someone who merely wants a spouse may tend to prioritize their own needs, overlooking the reciprocity required for a strong and equitable partnership.

Look for a partner who communicates with kindness and treats you with care. Such a person can be a partner in healing, helping to soothe past wounds and awakening the full potential of your character and spirit. Steer clear of those who bring turmoil and instability; they often cannot offer the commitment that fosters growth. Aim to connect with someone who embodies strength tempered with tenderness.

Sometimes, the paths of people in our lives diverge, not because they aren't meant to walk with us, but because the timing isn't right. Healing can demand solitude before two people can grow together. Letting go can be an act of self-love and a trust in life's timing. If a relationship is destined, it will find its way back when both are ready.

When someone becomes a regular part of your day and a source of joy, it's a sign of a deep bond. Their presence weaves into the fabric of your daily life, lifting your spirits. However, when the conversations pause, you might feel a void, as if something within you is missing, and an overwhelming sense of longing begins to take hold, making you yearn for their company and the comfort it brings. This feeling underscores the significant place they hold in your life.

Holding onto a friendship after a romance has ended doesn't make sense to me. If friendship wasn't strong during the relationship, it's hard to see why it would work without the romance. Relationships often hinge on being good friends first, and if that element was missing when we were together, it's unlikely to appear just because the love has gone. It's important to have a solid foundation of friendship in any relationship, and if that wasn't there to begin with, it's difficult to create it from the remnants of a broken romance.

The year is almost over and all I can say is, thank you... for all the lessons, blessings and experiences I've received.

I know I've moved on but sometimes when I think about you, when I think about us and our relationship... It still hurts. And yet, I've come to terms with it, but there's a lingering sadness in my heart.

Always remember, they chose to give you space when what you truly needed was affection. It's a poignant reminder that sometimes, people may not understand or provide what we deeply crave, even when our hearts yearn for closeness and connection.

Sometimes feeling the deepest kind of hurt comes from missing someone you still have strong feelings for, someone who used to send messages that filled your heart with warmth and joy. But now, you have to keep your feelings quiet, cherishing them from afar. It's like being pushed to turn the page on a story you never wished to finish.

I recently learned that stars, despite their brilliant glow, don't witness their own light. This reminds me of how individuals often fail to see their own growth, beauty, and the radiant change they bring to the world around them.

The one you gave your heart to entirely can sometimes be the very reason you become cautious about giving it away so freely in the future. Our deepest connections can teach us profound lessons, both in love and caution. But it's essential to remember that every relationship is a step towards understanding ourselves better. Each experience, no matter how painful, prepares us for a brighter and more authentic love ahead.

We often overlook the emotional weight that
comes with letting go of a relationship.
Choosing to part ways, even when it's for the
best, can bring a mix of sadness and grief. It's a
complex journey of balancing what's right with
the pain of leaving something familiar behind.

These days, some people expect you to demonstrate your value before they treat you with respect. This way of thinking doesn't sit well with me because I shouldn't have to prove myself to receive the treatment I rightfully deserve. From the moment you showed interest in me, you recognized my value. Let's be real and not play games. Mutual respect should be a given, not a reward. It's important to remember that genuine connections are built on trust and understanding, not tests of worthiness. Everyone deserves respect without conditions.

Some people grow up thinking that if someone
is mad at them, they don't love them anymore.
They might've learned this from family or old
relationships where people would just stop
talking when they got angry. But in good
relationships, it's okay to be upset sometimes.
What's important is to always remind each other
that even if there's a disagreement, the love and
commitment are still strong.

Always remember the times they pulled away when what you truly needed was their warmth and affection. It's moments like these that reveal a person's true intentions and the depth of a relationship. In times of need, genuine connections stand firm and unwavering.

Enduring trauma doesn't inherently grant strength. Instead, it can severely impact one's nervous system, affect digestive health, and trap individuals in a cycle of heightened alertness. Implying that someone is better off because of trauma overlooks the immense challenges and adaptations they've had to make just to keep going. Recognizing their journey means understanding the profound effects of their experiences, rather than romanticizing them.

Not everyone who has been hurt ends up hurting others. Some remember the pain they endured and can't bear the thought of inflicting that same pain on someone else. They understand the high emotional cost and choose empathy and kindness instead.

Instead of asking, "How did you miss the warning signs?", it's more compassionate to say, "I can see how much you wanted to be loved and valued." Recognizing someone's genuine need for affection and acceptance goes a long way in understanding their journey and choices.

It's important to offer understanding to those who find it hard to convey their emotions. Some hail from environments where their voices and feelings consistently went unnoticed. This struggle to communicate often traces back to earlier experiences of being overlooked or dismissed. Remember, each individual carries a story, and sometimes the most silent ones have faced the loudest storms in their past. Giving them patience and a listening ear can make a world of difference.

It's sad how frequently people are criticized for distancing themselves from those who forced them into a state of constant self-protection.

When someone talks about their solitude during their recovery, it's not just about the path to feeling better but also the moments when even a small act of kindness would have made a difference, but no one was there. Many who've faced hardships feel this way. They deserve understanding and admiration.

Being unaware of someone's intentions to harm doesn't make you gullible. You naturally trust and see the best in others, finding it hard to imagine causing them pain. Your kindness and understanding aren't flaws; instead, the issue lies in how they acted towards you. Recognize this and move forward with confidence.

After betrayal, the way we perceive someone can change dramatically. Their once familiar features may seem altered, reflecting the shift in trust and emotions. It's as if the actions have cast a new light on them, revealing sides we never knew or chose not to see before. Betrayal not only impacts our trust but also the very lens through which we view the person we once loved.

Before giving them another chance. Always remember how they made you feel when you were broken down by them. And always choose self-love above the ones who never choose you.

It's essential to respect and understand everyone's way of processing emotions. It's not our place to dictate how someone should or shouldn't express themselves. If they find solace in sharing their feelings on social media, support or simply scroll past. If their content doesn't align with your preferences, consider unfollowing. It's crucial to foster empathy and refrain from invalidating emotions. Embrace a mindset of understanding and kindness.

When you genuinely love someone, the idea of cheating doesn't even cross your mind. True love means respecting and cherishing your partner, and not causing them intentional pain. Breaking someone's trust is breaking their soul. If you find yourself unhappy, it's better to walk away than to betray their trust. Cheating is not an act of love; it's a clear sign of a lack of it. Simple as that.

You're not a second choice. Surround yourself with those who prioritize you. Remember, your worth is immeasurable, and you deserve to be with people who recognize and celebrate that every day. Stand tall in your self-worth, and never settle for anything less than being the first choice. Life is too short to be an option; be the decision.

You deserve someone who prioritizes your feelings and emotions, even if it means disappointing others. It's essential to have a partner who values your well-being above pleasing everyone else.

As I drifted off to sleep last night, my thoughts circled around the pure essence of genuine affection for someone. It's about desiring their presence in your life, driven not by what they can offer or achieve for you, but purely by the love you hold for them. It's in the little acts, like preparing a meal or crafting something special, not with the anticipation of reciprocity, but from the sheer joy of wanting to see them nourished and joyful. The beauty lies in the selfless acts stemming from an authentic heart.

From someone who's felt the weight of sorrowful nights, I'd like you to know this: You're not an inconvenience, nor a flaw, nor an issue. You are a unique individual filled with emotions, abilities, and endless possibilities. You have every right to joy, even in moments when you doubt it, and you're entitled to a promising tomorrow, even if shadows of yesterday loom large. Every stumble, every tear shed, every challenge faced is a testament to your resilience. Remember, your worth isn't defined by your darkest hours but by your ability to rise again. The world may sometimes seem indifferent, but your essence and potential are undeniable. Keep pushing forward, knowing that brighter days are on the horizon and that you have the strength to reach them.

Find beauty in the simple moments. When the morning sun casts a gentle glow through your window, let your words capture its essence, likening it to golden syrup. If such sights stir your soul, embrace them without hesitation. Applaud yourself for seeing the wonder in everyday things. Feel the rain as nature's gentle embrace. Pen tales about the moon's soft luminescence and the sway of petals in the wind. Weave magic into your narrative. Hold dear the imagery you create.

Always keep in mind that it's a natural human instinct to seek warmth, companionship, recognition, and love. It doesn't make you "excessively clingy" or "overly emotional" to desire that your emotional and social desires are fulfilled appropriately.

It's always possible to hit the reset button on your life. Consider wiping your social media slate clean. Imagine setting up a fresh profile that reflects your evolving music preferences. Picture yourself diving into studies or pursuing a career in a completely different city. Visualize forming connections with a whole new circle of friends. Think about adopting a brand-new fashion sense and a unique fragrance that speaks to the current you. Let go of the old parts of yourself that no longer fit. If you're feeling stuck or unsure about your next steps, remember that beginning anew is an option worth exploring.

When someone holds genuine love for you, they'll stand by your side, ensuring they never cause you intentional pain. They'll express remorse when needed, prioritize your well-being through sacrifices, demonstrate steadfast loyalty, and consistently show their commitment to you.

Until a person finds healing within themselves, they may bring toxicity into the lives of those who attempt to love them. This unresolved inner turmoil can manifest in various ways, affecting relationships and clouding interactions with mistrust, insecurity, and pain. It's crucial for individuals to address and work through their personal struggles, not only for their own well-being but also to foster healthy, loving connections with others. Until that healing occurs, even the most genuine attempts at love and understanding from others might be met with resistance and unintended harm.

Nothing is more attractive than a person who openly expresses their desire for you, demonstrates their deep affection, respects you, dedicates their time and focus to you, and strives to bring joy to your face. Such an individual is so engrossed in valuing and appreciating you that they see no one else in the same light. They prioritize open communication, ensuring that you always know where you stand in their life. Their commitment isn't just in words but is reflected in every gesture, every conversation, and every moment spent together, painting a vivid picture of genuine affection and dedication.

A genuine man operates with transparency. He'll share the truth about any topic you bring up, understanding that honesty fosters trust. He believes that when he's upfront with you, you'll have faith in him through thick and thin. This openness signals a man who envisions a future alongside you, one built on mutual respect and understanding. Such a man values communication and sees it as the bedrock of a strong relationship. He doesn't shy away from difficult conversations, nor does he keep secrets that might create barriers. Instead, he continuously works towards creating a partnership where both individuals feel secure, heard, and cherished.

Genuine love doesn't deceive, betray, fake, harm, or make you feel insignificant. It should act as a balm, soothing your concerns and fears. True love uplifts and cherishes, always offering a safe haven. In its embrace, you should find comfort and understanding, a place where vulnerabilities are respected and strengths celebrated. It's a bond that grows with trust and nurtures with kindness, ensuring that both individuals flourish together, feeling valued and cherished every step of the way.

It's alright to end things, begin anew, move forward, and say no. Being by yourself is fine too. However, what's not acceptable is remaining in a place where you don't feel joy, worth, or appreciation. That's not good for you. Life is too short to settle for situations that drain your spirit or make you feel less than. It's essential to prioritize your well-being and happiness. Sometimes, taking a step away, even if it's challenging, is the best way to rediscover your worth and reignite the passion and joy in your life. Always choose what's best for your mental and emotional health.

It's completely natural and human to want affection, interactions with others, attention, and love. You shouldn't feel like you're "asking for too much" or being "overly emotional" just because you seek to have your emotional and social desires fulfilled properly. Everyone has these needs, and it's okay to want them met.

A narcissist tries to make you believe that how you respond to what they do is the issue, but if they didn't act that way in the first place, you wouldn't react at all. They often deflect blame, making it seem as though you're overreacting or being sensitive, rather than taking responsibility for their own behavior. This redirection is a tactic they use to maintain control and avoid facing their own shortcomings. By making you question your reactions, they aim to keep the focus on you and away from their own actions.

Some folks are around just because they like what you do for them. They like that you're always there, making them feel safe, listening to them, and being dependable when things get tough.

It seems that what drew people to me wasn't my true essence. Instead, it was my consistent presence in their lives, my resilience in supporting them, and being a rock when chaos ensued. My perspectives ignited and enriched theirs, and I've always seen beyond imperfections, wishing only progress for them. My unwavering trustworthiness was a beacon. I've shaped myself into such a soul because I've yearned for a similar presence in my journey, encompassing kinships, friendships, and love.

People who realize they've wronged you often
keep their distance. It's as if they carry a weight
of guilt, and facing you becomes a mirror of
their actions. This avoidance is their way of
escaping the discomfort of confronting what
they've done. It's a silent admission of their
misdeed, a retreat from the responsibility of
making amends.

Don't feel pressured by set timelines or ages.
Whether it's moving out, settling down, starting
work, or finishing school, everyone has their
own pace in life. Life isn't about following a
checklist. It's okay to go at your own speed and
do things when you truly feel ready.

ROBERT M. DRAKE

When something bothers me, I go quiet. This is
my way of dealing with things. Instead of
getting mad or upset out loud, I like to think
about my feelings by myself. This helps me
understand how I feel and decide what to do
next. It's just how I handle things.

These days, it seems like everyone appears fine on the surface. But once you get to know them better and talk more deeply, you begin to see that many are facing challenges. It's like we're in a time where so many are putting on a brave face, sharing happy photos, but inside, they're trying hard to keep it all together.

When someone says one thing but does another, it's like they're playing tricks on you. And when they won't admit to it or make you feel like you're wrong, it's like they're making you doubt your own feelings and thoughts. This kind of behavior isn't just hurtful, it's damaging. It can make you feel lost, anxious, and really upset. It's important to remember your feelings are valid, and it's okay to seek help or talk to someone when faced with such behavior.

Choosing to be single, focusing on self-improvement, and holding out for someone who is genuinely excited about you is far better than settling for a person who is indifferent or uncertain about your relationship. Engaging in relationships where enthusiasm and certainty are missing can halt your progress, burden you with emotional baggage, and chip away at your self-esteem. These connections are merely drains on your time. To avoid the remorse of lost time and the hurt of neglecting your own needs, it's crucial to be selective and thoughtful about who you decide to date.

May you be surrounded by people who understand and manage their emotions well. People who face problems head-on, speak openly about their feelings, and don't resort to ignoring you or acting in hurtful ways. Wishing you companions who prioritize healthy communication and emotional understanding.

Some relationships give you the freedom to be yourself. They make you feel lighter and encourage you to pursue your passions. In these bonds, it's not just about being together; it's about growing, learning, and pushing boundaries. With them, every day feels like an opportunity, and you're motivated to explore more about yourself and the world. Such relationships are special because they don't restrict you; they inspire you to reach for the stars and be the best version of yourself.

If someone isn't actively choosing you, they simply aren't the right match. Rather than doubting your own worth based on their choice, see it as a clear sign of incompatibility and a cue to move forward. Continue this process until you find someone who genuinely desires you. The real drain in dating often comes not from the number of times you have to let go of unsuitable matches, but from the prolonged effort spent trying to turn ill-fitting connections into suitable ones.

Engaging in open dialogue about your desires, limits, values, and hopes won't push away a fitting connection. It's the challenging discussions that filter out those who aren't truly aligned with your journey.

A person who isn't right for you might make you feel like you're on your own, pushing you to discover your resilience and inner strength. However, someone who truly values you will recognize your capabilities and admire your independence. Yet, they'll stand by your side, ensuring you never face challenges alone, offering support even when you don't ask, and reminding you that together, you're even stronger.

For those trapped in circumstances they feel aren't meant for them, and the ones grappling to let go of a haunting past: My thoughts are with you. To the souls marked by past wounds, yearning for a love they're hesitant to accept, and to those feeling lost amid life's storms: know your worth is immeasurable. For everyone battling self-doubt yet brimming with untapped potential: I hope for a wave of comfort, tranquility, and restoration to embrace your spirit.

Sending hope to those grappling with situations
they sense aren't meant for them. For those torn
between leaving and staying. For souls bearing
the weight of past traumas, yearning for love yet
hesitant to let it in. To those who've drifted from
their true selves due to life's harsh tests and to
every individual doubting their immense worth
and potential. May every wounded heart find its
path to tranquility, restoration, and solace.

Healing can be incredibly challenging. Just when you think you're making progress, moving on, and working through your emotions, out of the blue, painful memories resurface. It feels like you're back at square one, navigating through those intense emotions all over again.

To everyone reading this: Kind-hearted souls do exist. In a world full of noise, there are still those who will pause, lend an ear, and genuinely understand your feelings. Some people are ready to admit when they're wrong and strive to better themselves. Seek out those who will uplift you, cherish your worth, and grow alongside you. Life's too short to be stuck with those who can't express their feelings or grasp the depth of yours.

If they are good to you. Don't talk about them behind their backs. Don't let others put them down in your presence. And don't think not even for a second they will betray you l, especially when you are not around.

Behind closed doors you treat her like shit but to
the world you claim to be absolutely in love with
her.

Just in case it goes unsaid today:

I notice you... battling obstacles, making your way amid the turmoil, and holding your ground.

Know that whatever hurdles you face, you
possess greater strength, determination, and
potential than you give yourself credit for.
Inhale deeply, relax your shoulders, let go of any
tension, and face the day at your own pace, even
if it's just one step at a time.

Often, when we feel like vanishing from the world, it's not that we truly want to fade away; instead, we deeply wish someone would see us and truly understand.

Healing can feel like an endless maze. Just when you think you're making progress, finding peace and releasing old wounds, a sudden memory or trigger pulls you back, forcing you to navigate through the pain once again. It's like climbing a mountain only to be pushed down and having to find the strength to climb back up.

If seeing her hurt doesn't touch your heart, her tears don't stir your spirit, and her sadness doesn't echo in your thoughts, then you have no right to say she means anything to you.

If causing her pain doesn't affect you, then don't
claim to care about her.

You deserve to be someone's first choice, not just an option. Surround yourself with those who value and prioritize you.

The last step to recovery is learning to set firm boundaries. As we heal, it becomes essential to protect our peace and prioritize our well-being. Sometimes, this means distancing ourselves from negativity or those who hinder our progress. By taking control of our environment, we empower ourselves to thrive and flourish.

Experiencing pain from someone you've bared your soul to is the deepest cut. Entrusting someone with your vulnerabilities and then being hurt is a profound betrayal. Yet, from these experiences, we learn and grow. Every setback carries with it lessons for a brighter tomorrow. Your wounds are evidence of your strength and the promise of better days ahead.

If you don't want her with anyone else, show her
she's the only one for you. It's that
straightforward. Cherish her, value her
uniqueness, and make her feel irreplaceable.
Every gesture, word, and moment should reflect
that she is your top priority. After all, the best
way to ensure she only sees you is by making
her feel truly seen and appreciated by you.

Some folks today remain single because they've found inner peace, making it hard for them to connect with those still struggling with past hurts. Choosing harmony over pain can make relationships tricky, as many people we encounter have emotional scars. Those who have healed look for wholesome connections. A lot of relationships we see are based on mutual hurt, where both partners lean on each other to fill their own emotional gaps.

For all the women finding their strength, always recall: it's better to have a moment of solitude than to share your space with the wrong person.

As time goes by, I've come to appreciate the art of subtlety and the wisdom in choosing my companions carefully. Being authentic doesn't mean granting everyone an insight into your world; it's about discerning who truly belongs there.

I've realized that true happiness comes when you release past burdens, regardless of their weight. What's done can't be undone. So, move forward. Even if you never received an apology or acknowledgment, free yourself. Holding onto pain only hinders you.

'Drive safely.'
'Look after yourself.'
'Have you had a meal?'
'Let me know when you're back.'
'Always here for you.'
'Morning!'
'Night!'
'I cherish you.'

Small gestures, but they reveal deep care and concern.

With age comes a longing for inner tranquility. You begin to value quiet moments and learn to let go of what isn't meant for you. The days of chasing after people or settling for less than you deserve start to fade, as you prioritize your own peace and happiness.

Be patient in understanding others. It's easy to rush into connections, but remember, appearances can be deceiving. People might present their best sides first. Set boundaries, learn to decline when needed, and always prioritize your well-being.

I wish you always remember the beauty you bring into this world. The way your laughter becomes contagious, the warmth you radiate that brightens every space, and the comfort you offer that makes people feel seen and valued. You're a beacon of positivity. While challenges will come, always hold onto this thought: the world treasures your presence immensely!

Believe me, no friendship or relationship is worth hurting your mind and well-being. That's it. It's essential to prioritize yourself and recognize when connections are more harmful than beneficial. Surround yourself with those who lift you up, not drag you down. Always remember, you deserve peace, love, and respect. Stand tall in your worth and never settle for less.

I stand by loyalty in relationships, not out of obligation, but from a deep respect for the bond of love. The idea of tarnishing someone's trust or causing them pain isn't in my nature. As we grow older, the importance of integrity in love becomes clearer. Betrayal isn't just a mistake; it's a choice that reflects immaturity. In every connection, respect and trust should be paramount. To consciously jeopardize that is not only a disservice to the other person but also a reflection of one's own character. True maturity is understanding the weight of our actions and choosing the path of honor and commitment.

I've learned that to be truly happy, we have to let go of old hurts. We can't change the past, so why let it hold us back? Focus on now and the good things ahead. Life's too short to get stuck in yesterday's shadows. Brighter days await when we step into the light of the present.

Flirting outside your relationship is a form of betrayal. Meeting up secretly is dishonesty. Engaging, messaging, or communicating covertly with someone when you're in a relationship is a breach of trust. The moment you find the need to hide, erase traces, or act stealthily, it becomes disloyalty. Infidelity isn't just physical; it starts with a mental drift, long before it manifests physically. Loyalty is more than just actions; it's also about intentions. Remember that.

When an individual repeatedly expresses or shows they're not prepared for a committed relationship due to past wounds, it's NOT a sign urging you to wait, mend their scars, or prepare them for a life with you. Instead, it's a CLEAR signal to establish limits and protect your emotional well-being. Relationships should be about mutual growth and understanding. It's vital to prioritize your own needs and find someone who complements your journey. Seek a lasting bond with someone who has worked on their healing, is genuinely enthusiastic about you, and is eager to craft a shared future together. Life is too short to anchor oneself to potential; instead, choose to sail with someone ready to navigate life's waves by your side.

A real man embraces empathy, values knowledge, and maintains unwavering commitment. Rooted in family values and heartfelt sincerity, he journeys through life with clear intentions. Financial wisdom, culinary prowess, and a commitment to tidiness define him. He is caring and attentive to the woman in his life, ensuring she feels valued and cherished. This individual rises to his duties with grace, championing justice at every turn. In a diverse and changing world, his legacy is one of goodwill, honesty, and esteem.

We all experience the pain of letting go. Missed chances, vanished hopes, and emotions that fade with time. It's a natural part of living, reminding us to cherish each moment.

Just like leaves fall from a tree, we must let go
of our past repeatedly.

For anyone needing to hear this: There are genuine, kind-hearted men in the world. Some who will not just hear, but truly listen, offering a shoulder and an understanding heart when you share your worries. They are the ones who embrace accountability, apologize sincerely, and remain deeply tuned into their actions and the ripples they cause in your life. Together, you and these men can embark on a journey of mutual growth, forging bonds of trust and understanding. They'll constantly remind you of your worth, making you feel treasured. Remember, you deserve a partnership filled with open dialogue, emotional depth, and unwavering respect. Never settle for less.

Many people desire long-term relationships, but
not all are prepared for the challenges, tears,
misunderstandings, and disagreements.
Relationships aren't like the perfect stories we
hear; they take effort and commitment. True
love means standing together through thick and
thin and finding solutions.

Over time, the dynamic has changed. Men don't always feel like the safe havens for women as they once did, and many women now seek comfort elsewhere.

Sometimes keeping it real.... Hurts.

Messaging someone else intimately is cheating. Offering someone else special attention is cheating. Making another person feel they have an opportunity with you is cheating. Cheating isn't just about physical intimacy. If you're giving someone else your time and focus, that's cheating. Just another form of it but wrong nonetheless.

There comes a time when every woman reaches her limit. She grows weary of the constant disagreements, the endless back-and-forths, and trying to grasp why she's being hurt. When she hits that moment, things change for you. She becomes indifferent, no longer feeling anger or resentment, just an overwhelming sense of nothingness.

Guys, you can't assume that a strong woman will always give you another chance! If you keep taking her for granted, there'll come a time when she loses interest. A time when your touch doesn't excite her, when she doesn't rush to pick up your calls, or when she stops seeking quality time because you've exhausted her emotionally. Be careful about taking for granted those who genuinely care about you. One day she might just realize her worth and her feelings for you might fade away.

Some guys don't grasp the depth of a woman's commitment. Even after facing many challenges in the relationship, she might still hold on, hoping things will change. Does she really want to jump into the unknown of a new relationship? Discover a different family culture? Pour her resources, dedication, and feelings into a new love? Experience closeness with another individual? Think again! She's looking for the man she's been with through every hurdle to step up and make amends.

True love is when someone thinks about your feelings. They notice the little things and always keep you in mind when making choices. In any relationship, you can tell how much someone cares by how much they think about you.

Heal the parts of you that hurt.... So that you
don't pass that brokenness to someone else.

Someone with narcissistic tendencies often tries to make you believe that the way you respond to what they do is the issue. However, if they didn't act in that way to begin with, you wouldn't have any reason to react. It's a classic deflection tactic. Instead of taking responsibility for their behavior, they shift the blame to your response. By focusing on your reactions, they divert attention from their own actions and avoid accountability. It's crucial to recognize this pattern and trust your feelings and perceptions, ensuring you don't get trapped in a cycle of self-doubt.

There are three essentials you should never feel
sorry for emphasizing:

When a man hasn't found healing within, he casts shadows on every love that comes his way. The unresolved pain and inner turmoil can cloud his actions and words, making it challenging for the women in his life to find the light. True love thrives in clarity and understanding, and without self-awareness and growth, he may unintentionally eclipse the warmth and affection offered to him.

For those who've found solace behind closed doors, hiding tears or moments of loneliness, my heart reaches out. If you've used artifice to mask your inner turmoil or gazed longingly, hoping to see someone else's reflection, know that you're seen and appreciated. And if ever you felt diminished by another's words or actions, understand that your value is immeasurable.

One profound guidance I once received was about breaking challenges down. When life seems too vast and daunting, narrow your gaze to the horizon just ahead. If that horizon still seems unreachable, look only as far as the next landmark. And when that feels too distant, just place one foot in front of the other. In those moments, I whisper to myself, "Keep moving forward," clearing the fog of uncertainty, knowing that with every step, things can change for the better.

For all those silently bearing the weight of the world on their shoulders, brighter days are on the horizon. Stay strong; you'll find your way through.

Remain unattached if you're someone who loves deeply, as it seems that such profound affection is often underappreciated in today's world. It's crucial to find someone who truly cherishes and reciprocates that depth of emotion.

If they make you a secondary priority, place them at the bottom of your list. Relationships should be built on mutual respect and valuing each other. If they can't give you the consideration you deserve, then perhaps it's time to reconsider their position in your life.

It's important to understand that, more often than not, people are aware of their actions and intentions. While it may seem like they're oblivious or unintentional, deep down, they often have a clear understanding of the choices they're making. So if someone fucks you over it's always almost certain that they knew exactly what they were doing and didn't care of the outcome. They didn't care if they hurt you, and they didn't care about what happened next.

One of the most challenging emotions is being caught in the limbo of uncertainty, torn between holding on and moving forward. It's like standing at a crossroads without a clear sign, wondering if patience will bring rewards or if it's time to seek a new path. Such moments of indecision can weigh heavily on the heart, but they also offer opportunities for deep reflection and growth.

Some people find it easier to let go than to mend what's broken. They might shy away from addressing issues or confronting discomfort, choosing instead to walk away. It's essential to remember that such choices often speak more about their own fears and insecurities than about the value they place on the relationship.

If you have a good relationship, cherish it. And by a good relationship, I don't mean a "perfect" one, but one where both parties genuinely try. There's effort, a strive to bring joy to each other, and continuous self-improvement. The bond isn't about embarrassing each other; it's about being confidants, always there to lean on. Sure, there will be slip-ups now and then, but if both are earnestly striving to be better for one another, love that bond, hold onto it, and celebrate its presence, because such relationships are rare gems.

In a relationship, communication is paramount. Getting upset when your partner expresses their concerns shows a lack of support. Rather than turning the tables and placing blame on them, inquire about any missteps and how to amend them. Even if it seems trivial to you, it's significant to them.

If you want your relationship to flourish, you should be prepared to distance yourself from individuals who make your partner uneasy. This isn't about control or toxicity. It's about maturity, respect, and prioritizing the bond you share above fleeting connections.

Life isn't just about the future. It's not solely about landing that dream job, living that perfect love story, embarking on that awaited journey, changing your appearance, or achieving a specific target. Your life is unfolding in this very instant. It's perpetually 'in the now.' So savor the present. Relish today and avoid being overly consumed with what's next. The reality is, the elusive 'tomorrow' never truly arrives. What you always get, each and every moment, is the gift of 'today'. We must always love today as if we might not be here tomorrow.

I wish you always remember the beauty that radiates from you. Think about the way your laughter brings joy to others. Consider the infectious vibrancy you bring that uplifts spaces and souls alike. Recognize the comfort and understanding you offer to those around you. Truly, you're a beacon in this vast world. Sure, challenges will arise. But through every twist and turn, keep this close to your heart: the universe cherishes your presence immensely!

In our home, we'll steer clear of harsh outbursts,
wild fury, or the sounds of doors banging or
glass shattering. There'll be no forceful actions
that threaten the very structure of our sanctuary.
Instead, our space will be filled with softness
and warmth. I promise to shield you from harm,
and you'll be my anchor, grounding me.
Together, we'll build a haven free from dread,
pain, or anxiety.

Give people the freedom and room they need.
Never beg for someone's presence. If they
choose to leave, let them. What's destined for
you will always return. Understand that journeys
can lead in different directions and individuals
may drift, but authentic bonds, if meant to
endure, will eventually reconnect. Respecting
the space and choices of others is a testament to
how profoundly you appreciate the intricate
dance of relationships and life's flow.

I don't hold any bitterness towards you, yet there are moments when I wonder if things would've been simpler had we just exchanged greetings and gone our separate ways.

Life is ever-changing. Sometimes, you face the loss of cherished relationships or parts of yourself that you thought would always be there. But before you know it, those missing pieces find their way back in unexpected forms. New connections blossom, and even more supportive friends arrive. Regardless of the tough times, brighter moments are on the horizon.

Cherish your own worth so much that you choose to step away from places where your worth isn't recognized or celebrated. Recognize that you deserve environments that uplift you and acknowledge your importance. Prioritize your well-being and surround yourself with those who truly see and honor your value.

ROBERT M. DRAKE

My best-friend once told me, 'There's no need to
fear starting a new chapter in your life.
Remember, this time you're not setting out with
an empty page; you're using the wisdom and
lessons from your past as a guide. Every past
challenge has equipped you with the tools and
insights for this new journey. Embrace the
growth and step forward confidently.'

Guys, you need to understand that constantly seeking another chance with a committed woman won't always work! If you keep taking her for granted, there will come a time when she no longer feels the spark. She may not eagerly answer your calls or seek your company because you've drained her emotionally. The joy she once felt in your presence might be replaced by indifference. Remember, even the most patient heart has its limits. Emotional wounds, if inflicted often, can change how she sees you. Constant neglect can fade the brightest of flames. It's crucial to recognize and respect the love and effort she offers. Because if you don't, there might come a day when you long for her warmth and find only coldness in return. Cherish the moments, and the genuine love she provides, for once lost, it might never return the same way again.

Perhaps we weren't destined for each other, but in my heart, I truly wished we were.

At times, it's essential to take a moment outdoors, refresh your mind, and reconnect with your identity and aspirations. Occasionally, you might have to explore beyond your familiar surroundings to truly discover yourself. As for my own journey, I find contentment right here, in this moment. All I desire is to be with you.

We once shared a love that was deep. But then,
you left me with a shattered heart.

Often, the most cherished memories carry a hint of sorrow, for we realize they're unique moments frozen in time, never to be replicated. Never to be relieved...and seeing it like that might be one of the saddest things alone.

Their fleeting nature makes them even more precious, like rare jewels that sparkle brightest in the dimming light of the past.

When encountering people who find it hard to articulate their feelings, it's important to be understanding and patient. Oftentimes, these individuals might have grown up in environments where their voices were overlooked or ignored, no matter how hard they tried to express themselves. This experience of not being heard can deeply impact their ability to communicate emotions as adults. Recognizing this, it's crucial to offer them the space and time they need to find their words. Their struggle to open up is often a reflection of their history, not their willingness to share. A little patience and empathy can go a long way in helping them break through the barriers built by their past.

Made in the USA
Las Vegas, NV
12 November 2024

11631954R00164